Dedication

This work is dedicated to every young mind determined to break free from the chains of miseducation. To the students who question, the teachers who empower, and the ancestors whose sacrifices paved the road we walk today.

May this guide serve as a light, a weapon, and a foundation.
Never forget — you were born to lead, not follow.
The world is your classroom. The truth is your legacy.

- Cedric A. Washington
Author. Educator. Revolutionary.

Who Lives Like This?! Publishing LLC
www.nerdyouthservices.org

ISBN: 978-1-970680-02-7 (Paperback)

Cover design and interior layout by
Who Lives Like This?! Publishing LLC Design Team

Printed in the United States of America

First Edition — 2025

THE MISEDUCATION OF THE NEGRO

IN THE 21ST CENTURY

HIGH SCHOOL STUDENT WORKBOOK (GRADES 9–12)

Teach Like Ced™ Series
Knowledge of S.E.L.F. (Social Empowerment Learning Framework)
By **Cedric A. Washington**

HOW TO USE THIS WORKBOOK

This workbook is designed to:

- be used **alongside the text**
- require **active reading**
- strengthen **critical thinking, writing, and analysis**
- help students develop **knowledge of self**

All responses should be **text-based** and **honest**.

PREFACE — STUDENT WORKBOOK

READING FOCUS

As you read the Preface, pay attention to:

- how education is described
- how systems affect teachers and students
- how culture impacts learning

KEY TERMS (FROM THE TEXT)

Write each word and explain it **in your own words using the reading**.

1. Education

   _____
   _____
   _____
   _____
   _____

2. Miseducation

   _____
   _____
   _____
   _____
   _____

3. Pedagogy

   _____
   _____
   _____
   _____
   _____
   _____

4. Culture

   _____
   _____
   _____
   _____
   _____

5. System

   _____
   _____
   _____
   _____
   _____

6. Compliance

_____
_____
_____
_____
_____

7. Intelligence

_____
_____
_____
_____
_____

8. Intelligence

_____
_____
_____
_____
_____

9. Knowledge

_____
_____
_____
_____
_____

COMPREHENSION QUESTIONS

1. According to the author, how does the academic system limit teachers?

2. Why does the author compare urban education to soul food?

3. What experiences led the author to believe schools prioritize models over expertise?

4. Why does the author say education can become a form of slavery?

TEXT-BASED ANALYSIS

Quote from the text:

"If you are controlled to do something that goes against your internal thought as to what is best, that's slavery."

Response:
What does the author mean by this statement? Use evidence from the Preface.

WRITER'S JOURNAL

Respond honestly. (Separate paper or google doc)

- What parts of school feel natural to you?
- What parts feel forced or disconnected from who you are?

CHAPTER 1 — PRIVILEGE (HS SW)

READING FOCUS

As you read, identify:

- systems
- access
- historical references
- who benefits and who does not

KEY TERMS (FROM THE TEXT)

Define using context:

1. privilege

_____
_____
_____
_____
_____

2. charter schools

_____
_____
_____
_____
_____

3. public schools

_____
_____
_____
_____
_____

4. miseducation

_____

_____

_____

_____

_____

5. constitution

_____

_____

_____

_____

_____

6. liberty

_____

_____

_____

_____

_____

7. justice

_____

_____

_____

_____

_____

8. psychological enslavement

_____

_____

_____

_____

_____

COMPREHENSION QUESTIONS

1. What role do charter schools play in urban education?

2. How does the author use Carter G. Woodson's words to support his argument?

3. Why is June 19, 1865 significant?

4. What does the author say privilege guarantees in America?

CRITICAL THINKING

The author writes that privilege creates two realities. (Separate paper or google doc)

- Describe those two realities using examples from the text.
- Who controls access in each reality?

WRITER'S JOURNAL (Separate Paper or Google Doc)

How does privilege appear in schools today?
Use examples you have personally seen or experienced.

CHAPTER 2 — FIGUREHEAD (HS SW)

READING FOCUS

Pay attention to:

- leadership
- authority
- obedience
- compliance

KEY TERMS (FROM THE TEXT)

1. figurehead

   _____
   _____
   _____
   _____
   _____

2. authority

   _____
   _____
   _____
   _____
   _____

3. leadership

   _____
   _____
   _____
   _____
   _____
   _____

4. compliance

_____
_____
_____
_____
_____

5. discipline

_____
_____
_____
_____
_____

6. school-to-prison pipeline

_____
_____
_____
_____
_____

COMPREHENSION QUESTIONS

1. What is a figurehead according to the author?

2. Why are Black principals often placed in impossible positions?

3. How does discipline contribute to miseducation?

4. What is the connection between figurehead leadership and the school-to-prison pipeline?

TEXT-BASED RESPONSE

Explain why the author compares figurehead leadership to Malcolm X's "House Negro."

WRITER'S JOURNAL

What qualities make someone a **real leader** rather than a figurehead?

CHAPTER 3 — KNOWLEDGE VS. EDUCATION (HS SW)

READING FOCUS

Identify:

- definitions
- differences
- who controls learning

KEY TERMS (FROM THE TEXT)

1. knowledge_____
   _____
   _____
   _____
   _____

2. education_____
   _____
   _____
   _____
   _____

3. intelligence_____
   _____
   _____
   _____
   _____

4. identity_____
   _____
   _____
   _____
   _____

5. cognitive
   dissonance_____
   _____
   _____
   _____
   _____

6. self-
   awareness_____
   _____

COMPREHENSION QUESTIONS

1. How does the author define knowledge?

2. How does the author define education?

3. Why is education without knowledge dangerous?

4. What role does identity play in self-awareness?

ANALYSIS

The author argues that mainstream SEL models lack cultural identity.

- Why is identity necessary for self-awareness?
- Use evidence from the text.

WRITER'S JOURNAL

What have you learned about yourself **outside of school** that school never taught you?

CHAPTER 4 — CULTURE = INTELLIGENCE = BEHAVIOR (HS SW)

READING FOCUS

Pay attention to:

- culture
- environment
- behavior patterns

KEY TERMS (FROM THE TEXT)

1. culture_____

   _____

   _____

   _____

2. intelligence_____

   _____

   _____

   _____

   _____

3. behavior_____

   _____

   _____

   _____

4. environment_____

   _____

   _____

   _____

5. rearing_____

   _____

   _____

   _____

   _____

COMPREHENSION QUESTIONS

1. What does the equation Culture = Intelligence = Behavior mean?

2. How does Willie Lynch's theory connect to modern behavior?

3. Why does the author say environment produces behavior?

CRITICAL THINKING

Explain how environment can shape intelligence using examples from the chapter.

WRITER'S JOURNAL

Describe how your environment has shaped the way you think or act.

CHAPTER 5 — PARENTS AND THE ENVIRONMENT (HS SW)

READING FOCUS

Identify:

- parenting
- accountability
- community influence

KEY TERMS (FROM THE TEXT)

1. environment_____
   _____
   _____
   _____
   _____

2. accountability_____
   _____
   _____
   _____
   _____

3. behavior_____
   _____
   _____
   _____
   _____

4. misinformed_____
   _____
   _____
   _____
   _____

5. community_____
   _____
   _____
   _____
   _____

COMPREHENSION QUESTIONS

1. How does the absence of Black fathers impact communities?

2. Why does the author say parents unknowingly contribute to miseducation?

3. What role did community accountability once play?

ANALYSIS

Why does the author say misinformed adults raise misinformed children?

WRITER'S JOURNAL

What responsibility do communities have in raising children?

CHAPTER 6 — HIP-HOP (HS SW)

READING FOCUS

Identify;

- culture
- influence
- responsibility

KEY TERMS (FROM THE TEXT)

1. Hip-Hop

_____
_____
_____
_____
_____

2. Culture_____
_____
_____
_____
_____

3. Influence_____
_____
_____
_____

4. Exploitation_____
_____
_____
_____

5. Narrative_____
_____
_____
_____
_____

COMPREHENSION QUESTIONS

1. Why does the author call Hip-Hop "the black CNN"?

2. How does the music industry resemble slavery?

3. What responsibility do artists have to their communities?

CRITICAL THINKING

Can music influence behavior? Use evidence from the text.

WRITER'S JOURNAL

What message does the music you listen to send about life?

CHAPTER 7 — POLITICS (HS SW)

READING FOCUS

Focus on:

- voting
- power
- unity

KEY TERMS (FROM THE TEXT)

1. politics_____
   _____
   _____
   _____
   _____

2. power_____
   _____
   _____
   _____
   _____

3. agenda_____
   _____
   _____
   _____
   _____

4. justice_____
   _____
   _____
   _____
   _____

5. unity_____
   _____
   _____
   _____
   _____

COMPREHENSION QUESTIONS

1. Why does the author say voting alone is not enough?

2. How have political parties benefited from Black voters?

3. Why does the author call for a Black agenda?

ANALYSIS

Why does political participation without organization fail?

WRITER'S JOURNAL

What issues matter most to your community?

CHAPTER 8 — THE BLACK CHURCH (HS SW)

READING FOCUS

Identify:

- faith
- control
- interpretation

KEY TERMS (FROM THE TEXT)

1. church_____
_____
_____
_____
_____

2. doctrine_____
_____
_____
_____
_____

3. interpretation_____
_____
_____
_____
_____

4. control_____
_____
_____
_____
_____

5. liberation_____
_____
_____
_____
_____

COMPREHENSION QUESTIONS

1. How has religion been used to control?

2. Why does the author criticize modern church leadership?

3. How does separation of church and state affect communities?

ANALYSIS

Why does the author say the Black church is the biggest culprit of miseducation?

WRITER'S JOURNAL

What should faith communities provide beyond inspiration?

CHAPTER 9 — REVELATION (HS SW)

READING FOCUS

Identify·

- truth
- history
- awakening

KEY TERMS (FROM THE TEXT)

1. revelation_____
   _____
   _____
   _____

2. miseducation_____
   _____
   _____
   _____

3. origin_____
   _____
   _____
   _____

4. correction_____
   _____
   _____
   _____

5. awakening_____
   _____
   _____
   _____

COMPREHENSION QUESTIONS

1. What is revelation according to the author?

2. Why is the four-hundred-year timeline important?

3. How does COVID-19 relate to revelation?

4. What must happen after revelation?

CULMINATING WRITING TASK

Prompt:
Explain how revelation disrupts miseducation and leads to empowerment.

FINAL REFLECTION

What is one truth you have learned about yourself or your community through this text?

www.ingramcontent.com/pod-product-compliance
Lightning Source LLC
Chambersburg PA
CBHW052118020426
42335CB00021B/2818